APOSTLE PAUL

Get to Know Series

Nancy I. Sanders

D1511118

APOSTLE PAUL

Nancy I. Sanders

ZONDERKIDZ

Apostle Paul
Copyright © 2014 by Nancy I. Sanders
Cover illustration © 2014 by Greg Call

This title is also available as a Zondervan ebook.
Visit www.zondervan.com/ebooks.

Requests for information should be addressed to:

Zondervan, 3900 *Sparks Dr., Grand Rapids, Michigan 49546*

ISBN 978-0-310-74473-3

Ronnie Ann Herman, Herman Agency

Cover design: Cindy Davis
Interior design: David Conn

Printed in China

14 15 16 17 18 19 /DSC/ 20 19 18 17 16 15 14 13 12 11 10 9 8 7 6 5 4 3 2 1

Dedication

To Dan — It's amazing to think that you were walking in the footsteps of Paul as I was writing this book. What an awesome journey God provided you to take! Dad and I thank God for you. We pray God will complete the good work He's begun in your life.

ACKNOWLEDGMENTS

First and foremost, I want to thank my husband, Jeff. As a fourth grade teacher, you always provide invaluable input into each one of my children's books, including this one! Thanks also to our wonderful sons Dan and Ben (and your new bride Christina!). Dad and I count our blessings daily because of each of you.

Thanks to Ronnie Herman, my agent extraordinaire! For your help, for your guidance, for your hard work, and for your love of birds and everything green and growing. You're a treasured gem in my life!

Also a big thank you to editor Mary Hassinger, Annette Bourland, and all the amazingly wonderful folks at Zonderkidz. What an exciting journey this series has been to work on together.

Thank you to Pastor Jack and Lisa Hibbs and for your commitment to speak the truth about the Bible and the teachings of Jesus Christ. I also want to thank Charlie H. Campbell, a frequent speaker at our church and the author of reliable information about faith, history, and the Bible. May the truth taught set the record straight about the trustworthiness of the Scriptures for this generation and those to come.

TABLE
OF CONTENTS

GET TO KNOW ... THIS BOOK

The Get to Know series is all about Bible heroes and the time period in which they lived. Each book in the series provides information about a person whose life and work impacts the world and Bible times. To help you understand everything in these books, we have provided features to help you recognize important information and facts.

BIBLE HERO
Look for a sandal for information about a Bible hero.

EYEWITNESS ACCOUNT
Look for a picture of an eye each time someone who saw what happened tells about it.

DID YOU KNOW?
Look for a clay jar to learn fun facts.

WORD BANK
Look for a scroll to learn the meanings of new words. The words are also in bold on the page.

Chapter 1

A BOY NAMED SAUL

Have you ever heard good news? Maybe you were invited to a birthday party or your Grandma called to ask if you'd like to go to the zoo. Or maybe you found out you were getting a new puppy.

Do you remember how excited you felt? What did you do? Did you hurry to tell all your friends?

Long ago, there was a man named Paul who heard good news. It was the best news ever. He wanted to tell everyone about it. After he heard the Good News about Jesus he spent the rest of his life traveling around, spreading that news.

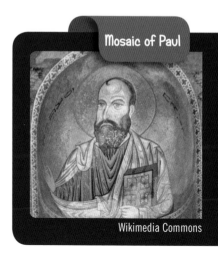

Mosaic of Paul

Wikimedia Commons

How do we know about this man Paul? He lived 2,000 years ago. For one thing, we know about him from **archaeological evidence**. Scientists called archaeologists have found many things from Paul's life. They have found cities he visited. They have found buildings he spoke in. They have found roads he walked on.

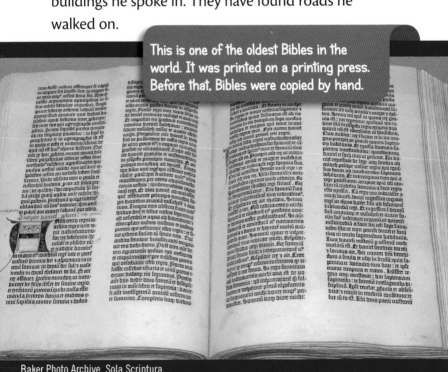

This is one of the oldest Bibles in the world. It was printed on a printing press. Before that, Bibles were copied by hand.

Baker Photo Archive. Sola Scriptura.

Archaeological evidence: Objects found that show the existence of people, places, and things

Most of what we know about Paul, however, comes from the Bible. There is a book in the Bible called Acts. It is part of the New Testament. And it tells us a lot of information about Paul's life.

Acts was written by a man named Luke. He was a friend of Paul's. Luke was an **eyewitness** to many things Paul said and did.

There are a lot of other books in the Bible that tell us about Paul too. These are letters Paul wrote that later became books in the Bible. We know even more about Paul's life from these books. Most important, from these books we know what Paul thought and believed about Jesus.

We know that Paul was born in the city of Tarsus. Tarsus was the **capital** of Cilicia. Today it is in the country of Turkey.

Tarsus was an important city in the Roman Empire. Many famous rulers went there. Julius Caesar, one of the most famous **emperors** in Rome, visited Tarsus. Cleopatra, the queen of Egypt, sailed there to meet Mark Antony, a powerful Roman ruler.

Tarsus was a major city for trade. Ships stopped

Eyewitness: Person who actually saw something happen

Capital: The city where the leader usually lives and rules

Emperor: The most important ruler of an empire

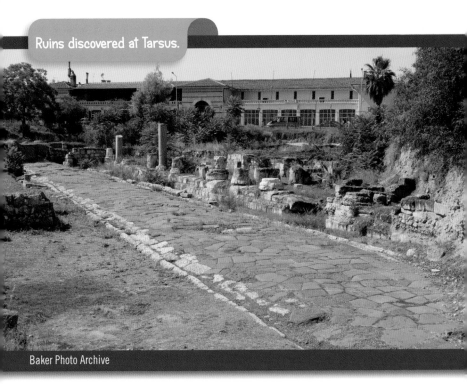

Ruins discovered at Tarsus.

Baker Photo Archive

near Tarsus along the coast. Traders traveled on land through Tarsus on their way to other parts of the Roman Empire.

Tarsus was also known as a city of great learning and culture. There was a university there. The **culture** of Tarsus was influenced by Greece as well as Rome.

Culture: The way a certain group of people dress and work and play

Paul grew up in Tarsus. As a boy his name was Saul. He had a **Hebrew** name because he was a Jew. Many people spoke Hebrew because it was the language of the Jews. The Old Testament was written in Hebrew. Many people also knew **Greek**. That was the language the New Testament was written in.

At that time, Jews lived in cities all throughout the Roman Empire. One of their **ancestors** was named Jacob. Jacob's name was changed to Israel by God. He had twelve sons. Each of those sons became a leader of one of the twelve **tribes** of Israel. Benjamin was one of the tribes in Israel. Paul was born into the tribe of Benjamin.

Paul was also a Roman **citizen**. This was very important in those days. Not everyone was. It cost a lot of money to become a citizen of Rome. But Paul didn't have to pay because he was born a Roman citizen. This made him even more important.

Hebrew: The language of the Jews, another name for a Jew

Greek: The language the New Testament was written in

Ancestors: Parents and grandparents and older people in a family

Tribes: Different groups of the same family

Citizen: Person who is a member of a country by law

DID YOU KNOW?

The Bible has two sections: The Old Testament and the New Testament. The Old Testament tells the history and beliefs of the Jews before Jesus was born. The New Testament tells the history and beliefs of Jesus and his followers. These are also known as the Scriptures.

BIBLE HEROES

Luke—Luke was a doctor. At times, he traveled with Paul. They went all over the Roman Empire to tell everyone about Jesus. Luke wrote the book of Luke and the book of Acts in the Bible.

Jesus—Many people believed Jesus was the Messiah. They believed he was God. These people became his followers. Some were eyewitnesses to his death and even saw him after he came alive again.

EYEWITNESS ACCOUNT

Like Paul, Strabo traveled all over the Roman Empire. He wrote about the different cities he visited. Of Tarsus, Strabo said, "The inhabitants of this city apply to the study of **philosophy** and to ... learning with so much **ardor** that they surpass Athens, Alexandria, and every other place which can be named where there are schools and lectures of philosophers."[1]

Philosophy: the study of truth and knowledge

Ardor: energy and strong feelings of liking something

DID YOU KNOW?

Critics used to think Luke was not a very good writer. They thought he made things up to put in the Bible. But now, information has been found that shows what Luke wrote is true. Bible scholar Charlie H. Campbell says, "More than eighty details in the Book of Acts have been confirmed by historical and archaeological research."[2]

Critics: People who do not agree with something

Chapter 2

A HEBREW OF HEBREWS

Jerusalem was the holy city of the Jews. King David made Jerusalem the capital of Israel. That was about 1,000 years before Paul was born.

David's son, King Solomon, built a temple in Jerusalem. The temple was the most holy place of all. It was where the Jews went to pray. They brought **sacrifices** to God at the temple. They celebrated important holidays that held deep meaning to their faith at the temple. These holidays are called **feasts**.

King Solomon's temple was magnificent. It was made of gold. It was one of the most beautiful buildings in the world.

Years went by. The temple was destroyed by armies

Sacrifices: Special gifts to God such as an animal or grain
Feasts: Important holidays celebrated by the Jews

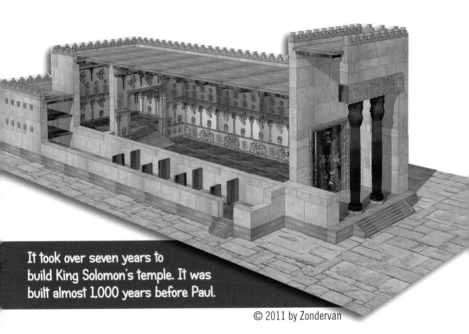

It took over seven years to build King Solomon's temple. It was built almost 1,000 years before Paul.

during battles. Then it was rebuilt. More years went by. The temple got old.

Finally, King Herod the Great decided to rebuild the temple one more time. By the time Paul was around, the temple was grand and glorious again.

When Paul was still young, he moved from Tarsus to Jerusalem. Paul lived right in the holy city of the Jews. He walked through the streets past tall Roman buildings. He saw Roman soldiers marching through the city or riding their horses. He went to the beautiful temple of the Jews.

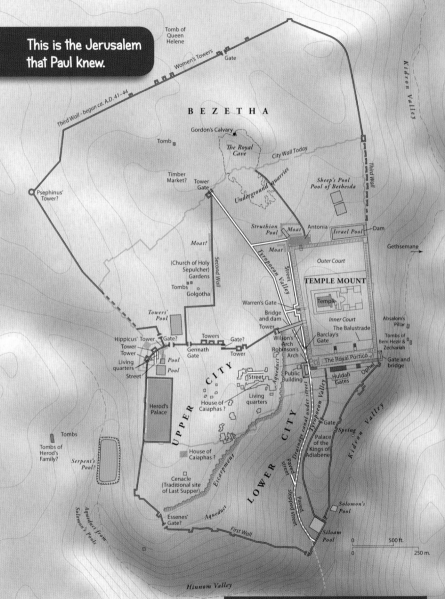

This is the Jerusalem that Paul knew.

Tomb of Queen Helene

Women's Towers

Gate

Third Wall – begun ca. A.D. 41–44

Kidron Valley

BEZETHA

Gordon's Calvary

Tomb

The Royal Cave

City Wall Today

Timber Market?

Tower Gate

Underground Quarries

Third Wall

Sheep's Pool
Pool of Bethesda

Psephinus' Tower?

Struthion Pool

Moat

Antonia

Israel Pool

Dam

Moat?

Moat

Gethsemane

Tyropoeon Valley

Street

Outer Court

(Church of Holy Sepulcher) Gardens

Second Wall

TEMPLE MOUNT

Temple

Tombs

Golgotha

Warren's Gate

Inner Court

Absalom's Pillar

Towers' Pool

Bridge and dam
Tower

The Balustrade

Barclay's Gate

Tombs of Beni Hezir & Zechariah

Hippicus' Tower

Gate?

Towers

Gate?

Wilson's Arch
Robinson's Arch

The Royal Portico

Gate and bridge

Tower

Gennath Gate

Tower

Ophel

Tower

Aqueduct

Huldah Gates

Living quarters

Pool

Street

Public Building

Street

Pool

UPPER CITY

House of Caiaphas ?

Living quarters

Tyropoeon Valley

Gate

Spring

Kidron Valley

Herod's Palace

Drainage canal under street

Palace of the Kings of Adiabene

Tombs

Tombs of Herod's Family?

Serpent's Pool?

House of Caiaphas ?

LOWER CITY

Paved street

Escarpment

stepped street

Solomon's Pool

Cenacle (Traditional site of Last Supper)

Aqueduct from Solomon's Pools

Essenes' Gate?

Aqueduct

First Wall

Siloam Pool

0   500 ft.

0   250 m.

Hinnom Valley

Paul went to school in a **synagogue** in Jerusalem like all Jewish boys. He was trained by a **rabbi**. He learned the Scriptures and the laws of the Jews.

Paul had a famous rabbi as a teacher in Jerusalem. His name was Gamaliel. Gamaliel was part of the Sanhedrin. The **Sanhedrin** was the highest group of Jewish leaders who met in Jerusalem. They made important decisions.

Gamaliel taught his students carefully. He taught them to study the Scriptures. He taught them about the history of the Jews. He taught them about the **traditions** they needed to follow.

In school, Paul learned the **Ten Commandments**. These are the main laws of the Jews. Paul read the **Psalms**. These are a group of poems and songs written

Synagogue: Building where Jews meet for worship

Rabbi: A teacher

Sanhedrin: The highest group of Jewish leaders who met in Jerusalem and made important decisions

Traditions: Ideas, words, or customs handed down from older people to younger people

Ten Commandments: Ten holy laws given by God to the Jews

Psalms: Poems and songs in the Bible written mostly by King David

mostly by King David. Paul studied Proverbs. These are the wise sayings of King Solomon.

Paul also learned about his **heritage**. He learned that Abraham was the first important

Wikimedia Commons

God wrote the Ten Commandments with his finger on two pieces of stone. God gave these to Moses.

leader of the Jews. In fact, Abraham was called the "Father of the Jews." Paul studied how Moses led the Jews out of Egypt. God delivered them from slavery and brought them to the land of Israel. Paul read all about the kings of Israel, and the **prophets**, the holy men who spoke God's words to the people. They all lived long, long before Paul was ever born.

Heritage: What is handed down from older people to younger people in a family

Prophets: People who tell God's words to others

In school, Paul also learned about the **Messiah**. The prophets wrote about the Messiah all through the Scriptures. The Messiah was supposed to come and save the Jews. It was a promise from God.

In Paul's day, many Jews hoped the Messiah would come and deliver them from the Romans. The Jews did not like Roman soldiers marching through their land. They did not like King Herod living in Jerusalem. They did not like the laws the Romans forced them to obey.

As he grew up, Paul learned the traditions and rules many of the Jews followed. Some of these were from the Scriptures. For example, the Scriptures said to eat some foods and not others. Other rules and traditions were not from the Scriptures. For example, they were

Statue of Roman soldier

Wikimedia Commons

Messiah: The promised deliverer of the Jews

supposed to wash their hands a certain way before they ate. Paul followed all these rules and guidelines very carefully.

Paul's father had been a **Pharisee**. Paul became a Pharisee, too, when he was old enough. By the time Paul was a young man he had become a very strong Jew. His faith and his heritage were very important to him.

BIBLE HEROES

David—David was Israel's most important king. King David made Jerusalem the capital of Israel. Scriptures said the Messiah would be a **descendant** of David.

Solomon—Solomon was a wealthy and wise king of Israel who built the temple in Jerusalem. He was the son of King David.

DID YOU KNOW?

Two-thousand-year-old scrolls were found in caves near the Dead Sea. These scrolls are known as the Dead Sea Scrolls. They were written in the days of Paul.

Pharisee: Jewish group who followed traditions they made up

Descendant: Person born of a certain family

THE TEN COMMANDMENTS

The Bible lists the Ten Commandments in Exodus 20.[3]

1. "Do not put any other gods in place of me."
2. "Do not make statues of gods."
3. "Do not misuse the name of the Lord your God."
4. "Remember to keep the Sabbath day holy."
5. "Honor your father and mother."
6. "Do not murder."
7. "Do not commit adultery."
8. "Do not steal."
9. "Do not give false witness against your neighbor."
10. "Do not long for anything that belongs to your neighbor."

PAUL'S EDUCATION

Paul told others about his schooling as a boy. In Acts 22:3 he said, "I am a Jew. I was born in Tarsus in Cilicia. But I grew up here in Jerusalem. I was well trained by Gamaliel in the law of our people."[4]

DID YOU KNOW?

The Jews were also called Hebrews. Paul thought of himself as a "Hebrew of Hebrews." He thought he was more dedicated to his faith than anyone else.

Chapter 3

DESTROY THE CHURCH!

When Paul lived in Jerusalem the city was full of well-known rabbis and teachers. One new rabbi was named Jesus. His teachings turned all of Jerusalem upside-down.

Jesus taught that the traditions of the Jews were not as important as the Scriptures said. Jesus' words upset many people. The Jews had developed these traditions over many years. Many of the Jews followed them carefully. Paul did too.

Jesus said he was the Messiah, the Christ. Jesus said he was the Son of Man. This upset many of the Jews in Jerusalem. Who did Jesus think he was?

And Jesus also taught his followers that he would

Christ: The Greek word for Messiah

Son of Man: A title Jesus used to show that even though he was God, he had come to earth as a man

Everyone in Jerusalem knew of the rabbi named Jesus. His teachings were different than anything people had ever heard.

'Jerusalem, Jerusalem', Tissot, James Jacques Joseph/Brooklyn Museum of Art, New York, USA/The Bridgeman Art Library

be sacrificed. This would pay the punishment for their **sins**. Only God could do that. What was Jesus saying?

Jesus did many **miracles**. Jesus healed sick people. He made a blind man see again. Jesus even brought dead people back to life. What was going on? All of Jerusalem was stirred up.

Did Paul see Jesus do any of these miracles? Was Paul in the crowds when Jesus taught them he was God? Did Paul hear Jesus teaching in the temple?

We don't know. But we do know the Pharisees in Jerusalem talked with Jesus many times. The Pharisees questioned him often. They were often upset with the things Jesus said and did.

Paul was a Pharisee in Jerusalem at that time. It was likely Paul did hear about Jesus and his teachings.

Paul probably knew what happened to Jesus next. The Jewish leaders had Jesus arrested. They took him to the **high priest**.

After being presented to the high priest, Jesus was sent to the Romans. Pontius Pilate was the Roman governor. Pilate sent Jesus to be killed. Jesus was nailed to a **cross** and died.

Sins: Bad things people think, say, or do

Miracles: Amazing events that only God could have done

High priest: The leader of all the priests

Cross: Two pieces of wood put together in the shape of a T that Romans used to kill people by hanging them on it

Most likely, Paul knew of all these things. Everyone who lived in Jerusalem heard about the death of Jesus.

But then something happened a short time after Jesus died. More news was heard about him. Reports spread around Jerusalem. His followers said that Jesus was no longer dead! They said Jesus had come to life again. Many people said they had seen him.

The followers of Jesus grew quickly in number. Within two months, more than 3,000 people said they believed Jesus was God. The early church was formed. The believers met often at the temple. [5]

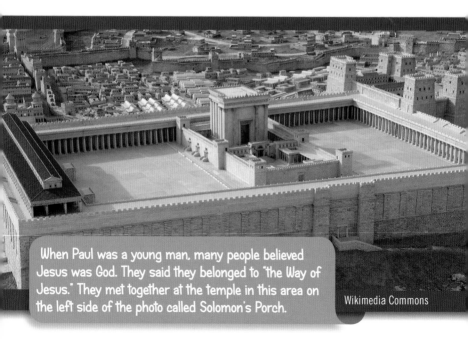

When Paul was a young man, many people believed Jesus was God. They said they belonged to "the Way of Jesus." They met together at the temple in this area on the left side of the photo called Solomon's Porch.

Wikimedia Commons

One day a believer was arrested. His name was Stephen. He was brought to trial before the Sanhedrin. Several **false witnesses** agreed to tell lies about Stephen. They said, "He says Jesus will change the practices that Moses handed down to us."[6]

The high priest questioned Stephen himself. Stephen answered the high priest. He told the history of the Jews. He said how long ago the Jews didn't realize God sent Moses to save them. And now they didn't realize God had sent Jesus to save them.

Then Stephen said, "And now you have handed him over to his enemies. You have murdered him."[7]

The members of the Sanhedrin were very upset at Stephen's words. They yelled at him! They grabbed him and dragged Stephen outside Jerusalem.

Paul was there. He kept watch over the coats of the witnesses. The men were so angry, they threw stones at Stephen. This was a common punishment given to many people who broke Jewish laws at the time. Finally, Stephen died. He was the first martyr for the Christian faith.

From that day on, Paul had a new purpose. He was

False witnesses: People who say they saw something happen but really didn't determined to stop Stephen's friends from spreading the news about this rabbi Jesus. Paul decided he would help bring an end to this new group. He was determined to destroy the church.

© 2013 by Zondervan

The stoning of Stephen.

Paul knew where to find the followers of Jesus. Many of them were Jews who lived in Jerusalem. He had probably known them for years. Paul went from house to house and had them arrested. He dragged these believers away, both men and women. He had them locked up in jail. He demanded they be put to death, just like Stephen.

The **persecution** of believers was terrible. Many of them left Jerusalem. They were afraid they would be

Persecution: Hurting or killing people because of their beliefs

killed. They also wanted to take the news about Jesus to other people in the Roman Empire.

Paul knew some of the believers were living in a city called Damascus. He was determined to arrest them too. So Paul went to the high priest. He asked the high priest for letters to take to Damascus. The letters would let Paul arrest these believers. He would bring them back to Jerusalem. He wanted them to be jailed and killed.

> The high priest was the most important priest of all.

Public Domain

Soon Paul was off on a trip to Damascus. He was going to destroy the new church as quickly as he could.

DID YOU KNOW?

There were two main groups of Jews in Paul's day. The Pharisees made many different traditions and rules to follow. The **Saducees** were very careful about obeying the Scriptures, but they did not follow the traditions of the Pharisees. The **Essenes** were a smaller group. People from that group wrote the Dead Sea Scrolls.

Saducees: Jewish group who was strict about following God's Law, but did not follow the traditions of the Pharisees

Essenes: Jewish group who wrote the Dead Sea Scrolls

EYEWITNESS ACCOUNT

Josephus became a Pharisee in Jerusalem at a young age, just like Paul. Josephus said, "I returned back to the city, being now nineteen years old, and began to conduct myself according to the rules of the sect of the Pharisees."[8]

BIBLE HERO

Stephen—Stephen was the first believer killed for his faith in Jesus. He was a **martyr**.

NEWS IN JERUSALEM

Paul probably heard how Jesus died on the cross. Three days after Jesus' death, two men met a stranger on a road near Jerusalem. In Luke 24:18, one of the men said to the stranger, "You must be a visitor to Jerusalem. If you lived there, you would know the things that have happened there in the last few days."[9] Later, the two men realized they were talking with Jesus as they walked to Emmaus. Jesus had come to life again!

Martyr: Person killed for his faith

Chapter 4

THE ROAD TO DAMASCUS

Paul left Jerusalem and traveled to Damascus. Some men went with him. He had the letters with him from the high priest, that gave him permission to take the new believers into custody.

Paul planned to visit the synagogues in Damascus. He wanted to find followers of Jesus in the city. Then he would arrest them and take them back to Jerusalem. Paul planned to lock them in jail and have them killed.

Finally, Paul was near Damascus. It was about noon. Suddenly, an amazing thing happened. A bright light shown down from heaven.

Paul fell to the ground. The bright light blinded him.

A voice spoke to him. "Saul! Saul!" the voice said. "Why are you **opposing** me?"[10]

 Opposing: Going against

Paul was shocked. What was happening to him? Who was speaking?

Paul asked, "Who are you, Lord?"[11]

"I am Jesus," he replied. "I am the one you are opposing. Now get up and go into the city. There you will be told what you must do."[12]

Paul's friends had to lead him by the hand. They took him into the city. He stayed in the home of a man named Judas. The house was on Straight Street.

For three days, Paul fasted and prayed. He didn't eat or drink anything. He was still blind.

What thoughts did he have during this time? Over the years, people have tried to guess. But nobody knows for sure.

Providence Collection/GoodSalt

Jesus appeared to Paul in a bright light.

Later, Paul wrote a letter to one of the churches about this time. He wrote, "With all my strength I attacked the church of God. I tried to destroy it."[13]

Visitors can still walk along Straight Street today where Paul stayed in Damascus.

But things had changed. Something astonishing had happened to Paul. He would never be the same. He had met Jesus, the man who died on the cross. He had heard Jesus' voice! Jesus was alive again just as the Christians had said.

Everything Stephen and the other believers said was true. Now Paul believed in Jesus too.

After three days, Paul had a visitor. His name was Ananias. The Lord had told him all about Paul. The Lord had told him to pray for Paul.

At first Ananias didn't want to do this. He knew Paul wanted to destroy the church. He knew Paul had come to Damascus to arrest believers.

But the Lord explained he had chosen Paul. Jesus said, "He will carry my name to those who aren't Jews and to their kings. He will bring my name to the people of Israel."[14]

Ananias obeyed the Lord. He found Paul and prayed for him. A heavy weight fell from Paul's eyes. Paul could see again.

Ananias baptized Paul. He was now a believer. Paul

Jan Smith/Wikimedia Commons, CC-BY 2.0

This is thought to be the house where Ananias lived in Damascus.

believed Jesus died to pay the punishment for his sins. He believed Jesus was God.

From that time on, Paul was a changed man. From that time on, Paul was ready to help change the world too.

BIBLE HERO

Ananias—Ananias saw a vision of Jesus. A vision is almost like a dream. In the vision, Jesus told him to pray for Paul. Ananias was very brave to go. He knew Paul had letters to arrest believers and take them to Jerusalem. But Ananias trusted Jesus. He found that Paul had really changed, just as he was told.

EYEWITNESS ACCOUNT

Jesus appeared to people many times after his **resurrection**. Paul also saw Jesus. In 1 Corinthians 15:3–8, Paul says, "Here is what it is. Christ died for our sins, just as Scripture said he would. He was buried. He was raised from the dead on the third day, just as Scripture said he would be. He appeared to Peter. Then he appeared to the Twelve. After that, he appeared to more than 500 believers at the same time. Most of them are still living. But some have died. He appeared to James. Then he appeared to all the apostles. Last of all, he also appeared to me."[15]

Resurrection: When Jesus rose from the dead and came alive again

> ## DID YOU KNOW?
> John the Baptist baptized people in the Jordan River. He lowered people in water and lifted them up again. Jesus' followers baptized people too. Baptism is a symbol of a believer's faith that shows God has washed a person clean from sin.

BELIEVING WITHOUT SEEING

Paul didn't believe in Jesus until he actually saw Jesus alive. Many people do believe in Jesus but have never seen him. In John 20:29, Jesus said, "Blessed are those who have not seen me but still have believed."[16]

> ## DID YOU KNOW?
> The book of Acts records Paul's **conversion** three different times. Each time, it is told a little differently. Critics have said this means the book of Acts isn't accurate or true. But other Bible scholars believe this helps prove the book of Acts *is* true.
>
> False documents would try to copy something exactly the same. But in real life, people tell about something that happened in different words each time they talk about it.
>
> The first time the book of Acts tells about Paul's conversion is when it is being described. The next time is when Paul is telling a large crowd about why he became a believer in Jesus. The third time is
>
> continued on next page

Conversion: The experience when someone decides to believe that Jesus is God

when Paul is talking to King Agrippa while on trial for his faith.

   In real life, Paul would naturally tell the story a little differently each time he talked about it. Many Bible scholars agree. This helps prove the book of Acts is an accurate historical document.

Chapter 5

PREACHING IN THE SYNAGOGUES

Paul had just heard the **Good News**. He heard that Jesus was the Messiah. And miracle of miracles, Paul heard the news from Jesus himself!

Paul had had an excellent education as a child. He had studied the Scriptures for many years. He knew about God's plan of salvation. He knew its history from the beginning.

Paul had read all the prophets' words about the promise of the Messiah. And now Paul was convinced that the promise had finally come true. Jesus was the Messiah. The blood from his sacrifice paid for sins once and for all. It was the best news Paul had heard in his entire life.

Good News: The news that Jesus is the Messiah, the Christ

Paul couldn't help it. He had to tell everyone about the Good News he had heard. His mission in Damascus had completely changed direction.

Paul started sharing the Gospel in the synagogues in Damascus. He told the Jews that Jesus was the Christ. He told them to believe in Jesus and they would be saved from their sins.

Everyone was shocked. They all knew why Paul had originally been traveling to Damascus. They knew he had been traveling there to arrest and kill the followers of Jesus.

Was this a trick? Was Paul pretending to be a believer so he could get names of people to arrest?

The people asked, "Isn't he the man who caused great trouble in Jerusalem for those who worship Jesus? Hasn't he come here to take them as prisoners to the chief priests?"[17]

But Paul didn't arrest anyone.

In fact, he spent time with the believers in Damascus. And his preaching became more and more powerful. He used the Scriptures from the Old Testament to prove that Jesus was the Messiah.

Gospel: Word meaning "good news," each of the first four books of the New Testament

Chief priests: A group of official Jewish leaders

This scroll of Isaiah is one of the Dead Sea Scrolls. This scroll told many prophecies about the Messiah.

Wikimedia Commons

This went on for quite some time. The Jews in Damascus became very angry. What was Paul doing in their city? They were so angry that they made secret plans to **assassinate** him.

The governor ruling over this area set up guards at the city gates. The guards watched the gates day and night. They planned to catch Paul and kill him.

But Paul heard about their plans. The believers in Damascus were now friends with Paul. They would help him escape.

One night, it was very dark. The desert air had cooled after the burning heat of the sun. Paul and his friends snuck through the dark streets of Damascus. They reached the city wall. There was a window in the wall.

Assassinate: Kill

Visitors to Damascus today can see the part of the city wall where Paul probably escaped.

One of Paul's friends had a large basket. The basket was big enough for a person to sit inside. Paul said goodbye to his friends. He quickly climbed into the basket. His heart pounded. He crouched down inside the crowded space.

Paul's friends pushed the basket out the window. They lowered the basket down. It landed gently on the ground.

Paul's life was in danger many times. He escaped from Damascus at night in a basket lowered over the city wall.

© by Zondervan

Paul peeked out of the basket. Nobody had seen him! He climbed out and ran off into the darkness. He was safe.

Paul decided to go back to Jerusalem. It had been three years since he had left. He wanted to meet Peter, a leader of the new church, and get to know him and his faith.

Paul tried to join the believers in Jerusalem. They were afraid of him. They remembered how he had arrested believers the last time he was in the city. They didn't trust Paul at all.

Finally, a man named Barnabas listened to Paul. He believed Paul really was a changed man. Barnabas and Paul became friends.

Barnabas introduced Paul to Peter and the other apostles. Barnabas told them how Jesus had appeared to Paul on the road to Damascus. Barnabas told them how Paul had preached in the synagogues there.

Paul visited Peter in Jerusalem. These ruins are the location of Peter's house in Galilee.

www.HolyLandPhotos.org

After that, Paul stayed at Peter's house for fifteen days. While he was there, he even visited with James, the brother of Jesus.

Paul wanted to share the Good News with everyone in Jerusalem. He preached with boldness. He talked about Jesus with the Jews. He even argued with them. They became so angry with Paul they wanted to kill him.

The believers in Jerusalem heard about the Jewish leaders' plans. They were now Paul's friends. So they helped him escape from Jerusalem. They **escorted** him safely to the city of Caesarea. Then they sent him off to Tarsus.

After many years away from home, Paul was going back to Tarsus. When he left Tarsus, he was a normal Jewish boy. Now he was a believer in Jesus, the Christ.

What new adventures would Paul have?

EYEWITNESS ACCOUNT

Damascus was a prosperous city when Paul lived there. It had a rich history. Strabo said in his book, "Damascus is a considerable city, and in the time of the Persian Empire was nearly the most distinguished place in that country."[18]

DID YOU KNOW?

After Paul's conversion, he went away for a while to Arabia. Perhaps he visited Mount Sinai, where God gave Moses the Ten Commandments. Perhaps he studied the Scriptures to learn more about Jesus, the Messiah. Nobody knows for sure what he did. But after that, he went back to Damascus and then went on to Jerusalem.

Escorted: When someone goes with a person to keep them safe

BIBLE HEROES

Peter—Peter was one of the twelve disciples of Jesus. After the resurrection of Jesus, Peter and the other disciples were called apostles. Peter and the apostles were the leaders of the early church.

James—James was the brother of Jesus. He was a leader of the church in Jerusalem. He wrote the book of James in the Bible.

THE MESSIAH

Paul used the Old Testament to show that Jesus was the Messiah. Isaiah 53:4–5 says, "He suffered the things we should have suffered. He took on himself the pain that should have been ours. But we thought God was punishing him. We thought God was wounding him and making him suffer. But the servant was pierced because we had sinned. He was crushed because we had done what was evil. He was punished to make us whole again. His wounds have healed us."[19]

Chapter 6

CHRISTIANS: FOLLOWERS OF CHRIST

Paul moved back to his childhood hometown of Tarsus. He worked as a tentmaker to earn money for food and a place to live. These tents were made from fabric woven from goat hair.

Not much else is known about Paul during these years. But one day, Paul's friend Barnabas arrived in Tarsus.

Barnabas had interesting news to share. He told Paul a lot of believers had left Jerusalem when Stephen was killed for his faith. They had moved to different parts of the Roman Empire. Some of them had moved to Cyprus. Others had moved to Antioch.

At first, these believers shared the Good News about Jesus only with other Jews. But soon they

Goats with long hair live in the mountains near Tarsus. People use this goat hair to make cloth for tents.

Baker Photo Archive

started to tell it to **Gentiles**, people who weren't Jews. Soon, a large number of people especially in Antioch believed that Jesus was God.

The apostles in Jerusalem heard about what was

Gentiles: People who aren't Jews

happening in Antioch. They sent Barnabas there to help. Barnabas taught the new believers to stay close to the truth. Even more people in Antioch became believers.

Barnabas invited Paul to come help him with the church at Antioch. Paul was happy to go. He remembered the message Jesus had given him in Damascus. Jesus had told him he would carry his name "to those who aren't Jews and to their kings."[20]

Paul went with Barnabas to Antioch. They

Paul began all three of his missionary journeys from Antioch.

Todd Bolen/www.BiblePlaces.com

met with the people there for a whole year. Paul was very busy teaching. They had so much to learn! They didn't know the Scriptures at all. Many of them had grown up worshiping **idols**. Idols were statues

Idols: Statues that people worship

people thought were gods. Many of them had never heard of a Messiah. Many of them didn't know about God's plan to take care of the sin problem. Large numbers of people heard the message

Wikimedia Commons

Paul and Barnabas worked together to share the Gospel with people who weren't Jews.

about Jesus. People started calling the new believers "**Christians.**" This meant they were followers of Christ. They accepted Jesus as their Lord and **Savior.** They wanted to learn more and more about God's love.

At one point, a group of prophets came from Jerusalem. One man was named Agabus. He said there would soon be a **famine** in the Roman Empire.

Christians: People who believe in Jesus Christ and his teachings

Savior: The One who saves people from getting punished for their sins

Famine: When a place has no food

Money was collected to help the Christians in that area. Paul and Barnabas were sent to take the gift to Jerusalem.

Paul and Barnabas traveled to Jerusalem with the money. They met with Peter, James, and John. Paul shared how God called him to be an apostle to the Gentiles. They gave their approval to his work.

Paul and Barnabas then returned to Antioch. They took a young cousin of Barnabas with them. His name was John Mark. He was also known as Mark and sometimes John.

One day, the prophets and teachers in Antioch were gathered together. They were fasting and worshiping the Lord.

The **Holy Spirit** spoke to them. "Set apart Barnabas and Saul for me," he said. "I have appointed them to do special work."[21]

They fasted and prayed even more. Then the leaders knew what to do. They sent Paul and Barnabas on a journey. Paul and Barnabas would be **missionaries**. They would travel and take the message of Jesus with them. They would go to other places in the Roman Empire.

Holy Spirit: The Spirit of God

Missionaries: People who take a message of faith to others

BIBLE HERO

Barnabas—Barnabas was one of the early church leaders. He was also a friend of Paul's. Barnabas went to the new church at Antioch to teach them the Scriptures and the true message about Jesus. Barnabas brought Paul to Antioch to help with the new church.

DID YOU KNOW?

Antioch was the third biggest city in the Roman Empire. Rome was the largest city. It was the capital of the Roman Empire. Next came Alexandria, the capital of Egypt. After that came Antioch.

EYEWITNESS ACCOUNT

Strabo told about the important city of Antioch in his book. Strabo wrote, "Antioch is the **metropolis** of Syria. A palace was constructed there for the princes of the country."[22]

BIBLE HERO

Agabus—Agabus was a prophet during New Testament times. He brought two important messages from God. The first was a prediction of a famine. The second came many years later. He predicted Paul would be arrested in Jerusalem. Both came true.

Metropolis: The main city of an area

Chapter 7

THE FIRST MISSIONARY JOURNEY

Paul and Barnabas set out on an exciting adventure together. John Mark, the young cousin of Barnabas, went along to help them. Their mission: to spread the Good News about Jesus Christ. First to the Jews. Then to the Gentiles.

They left Antioch and went to a port city on the **Mediterranean Sea**. They bought tickets and sailed to the island of Cyprus. Barnabas was from Cyprus. He felt like he was going home.

Each Saturday while there, they attended the local synagogue. As visitors, they would have been invited to stand up and teach about the Scriptures.

They used the Old Testament to talk about the

Mediterranean Sea: A large body of water surrounded by countries in the Roman Empire during Paul's day

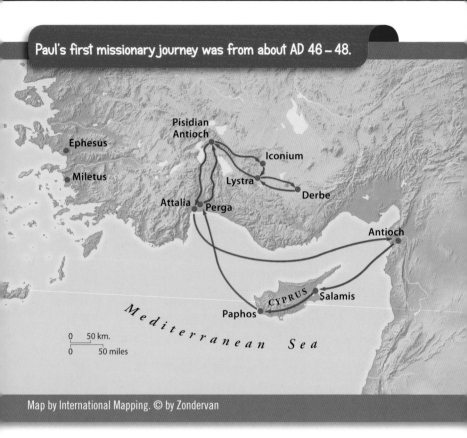

Paul's first missionary journey was from about AD 46 – 48.

Map by International Mapping. © by Zondervan

promise of the Messiah. They shared how Jesus was the answer to that promise. They explained he was the Messiah, the **Son of God**.

After Cyprus, the three men traveled to the other

Son of God: A title for Jesus meaning he is the Messiah

side of the island. They went to Paphos. It was another important city. The Roman governor of this region lived there. His name was Sergius Paulus.

The Roman governor heard that Paul and Barnabas were visiting. He invited them to come and share their message with him.

Paul and his friends arrived at the governor's home. Paul spoke boldly to him.

As Paul spoke, however, trouble started. The governor had a servant named Elymas. He was a Jew. He was also a magician.

Elymas did not want the governor to become a Christian. He spoke out against Paul and his message.

Paul saw what the magician was doing. He looked at him and said, "You are a child of the **devil**! You are an enemy of everything that is right! You cheat people. You use all kinds of tricks. Won't you ever stop twisting the right ways of the Lord?"[23]

Next Paul said an amazing thing to the magician. Paul said, "Now the Lord's hand is against you. You are going to go blind. You won't be able to see the light of the sun for a while."[24]

Devil: Satan, the enemy of God and the spirit of evil

Immediately, Elymas became blind. God had worked a miracle through Paul.

The governor heard what Paul had said about Jesus. He saw that his servant was now blind. The governor was so amazed that his heart was changed. He decided to believe that Jesus was God.

This was one of the first times an important Roman ruler became a Christian. This showed Paul that he really was supposed to take the Gospel to the Gentiles too. From then on, Paul no longer went by his Hebrew name Saul. From then on, everyone called him by his Greek name Paul.

Paul and his friends left the island of Cyprus. They sailed to the city of Perga. For some reason, John Mark deserted them at this point in the trip.

Bible scholars aren't quite sure why he left. Was he sick? Did he miss home? Did Barnabas decide it was too dangerous to have him along? Did John Mark think that Paul should not be sharing the Good News with the Gentiles? Nobody knows for sure. But John Mark went home to Jerusalem.

Paul and Barnabas continued to travel from city to city, preaching and teaching about Jesus. At one place, almost the whole city came out to hear their message!

Many Jews were getting angry. They complained to the leaders of their cities. They tried to get Paul and

Barnabas killed. Paul and Barnabas faced constant danger.

These towers can still be seen in Perga today.

But this did not stop the men. Some of the Jews did become believers that Jesus was the Messiah, however. And a great number of Gentiles became Christians. Paul and Barnabas started new churches everywhere they went.

In the city of Lystra, Paul healed a man who couldn't walk. The crowds were amazed. They thought Barnabas was the god Zeus. They thought Paul was the god Hermes. The crowds tried to worship Paul and Barnabas. They wanted to sacrifice animals to them.

Paul and Barnabas felt terrible. "Turn away from these **worthless** things," they shouted to the crowds. "Turn to the living God. He is the one who made the

Wikimedia Commons

heavens and the earth and the sea. He made everything in them."[25]

Soon some Jews arrived on the scene. They had heard Paul and Barnabas speak in other cities. They told the crowds to kill Paul.

Statue of the Greek god Zeus.

People threw stones at him. Finally, they thought Paul was dead. They dragged him out of the city.

But Paul was not dead! The Christians gathered around him. They prayed for him. Paul got up and went with his friends back into Lystra. The next day Paul and Barnabas left for

Worthless: Having no use at all

the city of Derbe. They continued to preach the Gospel as they went.

Statue of the Greek god Hermes.

Finally, Paul and Barnabas were ready to go home. They turned around and went back to most of the cities they had just visited. They went to each of the new churches they had established. They appointed leaders in each church community.

Then they sailed back home to Antioch. Their first missionary journey had come to an end.

BIBLE HERO

John Mark—John Mark was still a young man when he traveled with Paul and Barnabas. At times, he traveled with Peter. When he was older, he wrote the Gospel of Mark from the Bible. It is the second book in the New Testament.

DID YOU KNOW?

Paul and some of the other apostles did miracles. The power of the Holy Spirit worked through them to do this. Many people believed in Jesus because of these miracles.

PAUL'S MESSAGE

Paul's message was the same everywhere he went. In Acts 13:38–39, Paul said, "My brothers, here is what I want you to know. I announce to you that your sins can be forgiven because of what Jesus has done. Through him everyone who believes is made right with God."[26]

THE MESSAGE SPREADS

In Acts 1:8, Jesus said to his followers, "But you will receive power when the Holy Spirit comes on you. Then you will be my witnesses in Jerusalem. You will be my witnesses in all Judea and Samaria. And you will be my witnesses from one end of the earth to the other."[27] Paul and Barnabas followed Jesus' instructions when they went on their first missionary journey together. They were taking the Gospel all over the Roman Empire.

Chapter 8

THE JERUSALEM COUNCIL

Paul and Barnabas were happy to be in Antioch. It was their home church. They shared about their first missionary journey. Everyone was glad to hear the news.

One day, visitors arrived at their church. These visitors began to teach a new idea to the Christians. They said people could not be saved just by believing Jesus was God. They said people could only be saved if they obeyed certain rules too.

"Moses commanded you to be **circumcised**," they said. "If you aren't, you can't be saved."[28]

Paul and Barnabas did not agree with this new teaching. They argued with the visitors.

 Circumcised: A surgery sometimes given to baby boys

The church leadership at Antioch made a decision. They decided to send Paul and Barnabas to Jerusalem. They would ask the heads of the church this question. Was **salvation** a free gift? Or did people need to follow rules or do something extra to earn salvation?

Ancient Antioch lies underneath the modern city of Antakya today.

Salvation: Saving from punishment for sins

Paul and Barnabas traveled to Jerusalem. They met with other believers. They reported how the church in Antioch had grown. They told about the things that happened on their first missionary journey. They said how both Jews and non-Jews were being saved.

Then, some of the Christians stood up. They were

The apostle Paul may have walked on this road at the end of his walk from Alexandria Troas to Assos. It was here at Assos that he reconnected with his party and set sail for Mitylene (on his way back to Jerusalem).

www.HolyLandPhotos.org

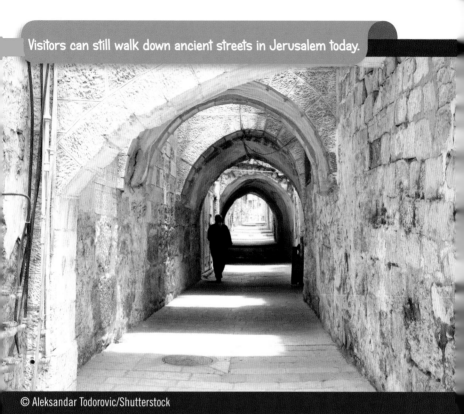

Visitors can still walk down ancient streets in Jerusalem today.

© Aleksandar Todorovic/Shutterstock

Pharisees. They said, "Those who aren't Jews must be circumcised. They must obey the **Law of Moses**."[29]

This was the exact thing Paul and Barnabas had come to talk about.

Law of Moses: The first five books in the Bible that include the Ten Commandments

An important meeting was called. Today this meeting is known as the **Jerusalem Council**. The apostles were there, including Peter. James, the brother of Jesus, Paul, and Barnabas were there too.

Everyone talked about this new teaching. Was salvation a gift? Could it be given by **God's grace** just because people decided to trust in Jesus to save them? Or did people need to do something else to be saved?

Finally, Peter stood up. He shared how God had chosen him to talk with people who weren't Jews. Peter had told them about Jesus. Even while he was speaking, many people decided to believe in Jesus. God had given them the Holy Spirit.

Peter now said to the Jerusalem Council, "Now then, why are you trying to test God? You test him when you put a heavy load on the believers' shoulders. Our people of long ago could not carry that load. We can't either. No! We believe we are saved through the grace of our Lord Jesus. Those who aren't Jews are saved in the same way."[30]

Jerusalem Council: A special meeting of the early church that decided salvation was a gift from God to those who believe in Jesus

God's grace: Giving the gift of salvation without following rules to earn it

Next, Paul and Barnabas spoke. They agreed with Peter's words.

Then, James spoke. He was now a leader of the church in Jerusalem. James used the Bible as the final authority to answer the question.

James spoke words from the book of Amos, a book in the Old Testament. The book of Amos said how God cares about both the Jews and the non-Jews. Amos said how God chose some of both to be his very own people.

James said, "We should not make it hard for the non-Jews who are turning to God."[31] Then James suggested a letter be written and taken to the new believers.

The letter would ask the non-Jews to respect some of the laws about food that the Jews followed. This way the believers, both Jews and non-Jews, could all eat at the same table when they met together. The letter would also ask the non-Jews to live pure lives and not do bad things.

One thing the letter did not say was that people had to follow rules to get saved. The leaders at the Jerusalem Council all agreed. Salvation was a true gift. Everyone who trusted in Jesus would be saved.

This decision was a turning point in the history of the church. It was official. The work Jesus did and his death on the cross paid completely for our sins. Nothing else anybody could do could pay that price.

When people chose to believe this, they would be saved. Their sins would be forgiven. They would be made right with God. They would live forever in heaven with God after they died.

In later years, **false teachers** would come along and teach different things about salvation. They would say there were certain rules to follow in order to be saved. They would start new churches. Some would call themselves Christians. But the members of their churches would have to follow their rules to be saved.

At the Jerusalem Council, the decision was clear. No special rules had to be followed to be saved. Ever.

Paul and Barnabas could not know how important the Jerusalem Council's decision would become to the church. But they knew the right decision had been made. They took the message back to their church in Antioch. Two men, Judas and Silas, went with them.

Paul and Barnabas stayed in Antioch for awhile. Then one day, Paul said to Barnabas, "Let's go back to all the towns where we preached the Word of the Lord. Let's visit the believers and see how they are doing."[32]

Paul's second missionary journey was about to begin.

False teachers: People who taught things the Bible did not teach

BIBLE HERO

Amos—Amos was a shepherd during Old Testament times. God called him to be a prophet. He wrote the book of Amos in the Bible.

DID YOU KNOW?

Peter and his Jewish friends knew the Gospel was for everyone, not just Jews. Peter told a Roman commander about Jesus. His name was Cornelius. He and many others in his house became Christians. God gave them the Holy Spirit.

GOD'S GRACE

Paul believed in God's grace. In Romans 3:22–24, Paul said, "We are made right with God by putting our faith in Jesus Christ. That happens to all who believe. It is no different for the Jews than for anyone else. Everyone has sinned. No one measures up to God's glory. The free gift of God's grace makes all of us right with him. Christ Jesus paid the price to set us free. God gave him as a sacrifice to pay for sins. So he forgives the sins of those who have faith in his blood."[33]

BIBLE HERO

Silas—Silas left Jerusalem and went to Antioch with Paul and Barnabas. Later, Silas traveled with Paul on his second missionary journey.

Chapter 9

THE SECOND MISSIONARY JOURNEY

Paul wanted to travel back to the churches they started on their first trip. Barnabas thought this was a good idea.

Barnabas suggested giving John Mark another chance. He wanted to take his young cousin on the trip with them.

Paul didn't think this was wise. John Mark had deserted them before. Would he leave them again?

Barnabas and Paul could not agree about what to do.

Finally, it was decided. There would be two missionary trips. Barnabas and John Mark would sail to Cyprus. They would visit the church there. Paul and his friend Silas would follow the road north. They would visit those churches.

Not much is known about Barnabas and John Mark's trip. But the book of Acts tells about the trip

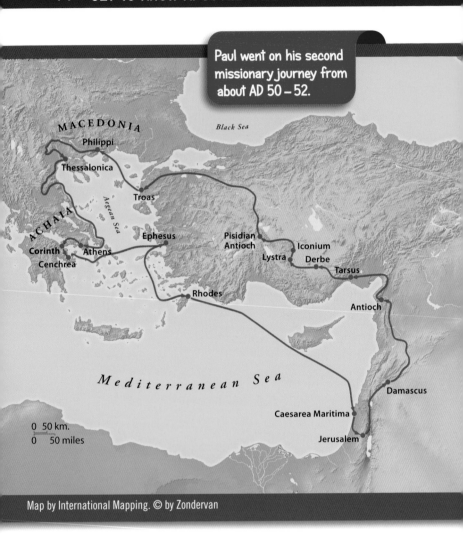

Paul went on his second missionary journey from about AD 50 – 52.

Map by International Mapping. © by Zondervan

Paul and Silas took. They headed over land to the cities of Derbe and Lystra.

They met with Christians in churches Paul started

on his first journey. Paul shared the letter from James and the Jerusalem Council with them. He encouraged the believers to follow the truth.

A young believer named Timothy lived in Lystra. His mother was Eunice and his grandmother was Lois. They were both Christians. They probably became Christians when Paul and Barnabas first visited the city.

Paul decided to invite Timothy to join him on his trip. Paul felt Timothy would be a strong leader. He was a good teacher and would be a valuable helper to Paul and Silas.

In another city, Luke joined the missionary team. They traveled together to the city of Philippi, an important city in the Roman Empire.

It seems this city did not have a synagogue. So Paul and his team went to a place by the river. Women gathered there for prayer. Paul and his team spoke to the women about Jesus. One of the women was Lydia.

Lydia heard Paul's message. She decided to become a Christian. So did her family. They were baptized. Then Lydia invited Paul and his team to stay at her house.

They stayed in the city for a number of days. They shared the Gospel with many people.

However, there was a problem. One woman followed them around who was a slave. She had an evil spirit from the devil inside her. This spirit helped her to tell people's fortunes. She earned a lot of money for her owners as a **fortune teller.**

One day Paul spoke to the evil spirit. Paul said, "In the name of Jesus Christ, I command you to come out of her!"[34]

The evil spirit left immediately.

Now the slave owners were upset. They couldn't make money if their slave wasn't telling people's fortunes! They grabbed Paul and Silas. They dragged them to the city's judges. The owners said, "These men are Jews. They are making trouble in our city."[35]

Paul and Silas were whipped. Then they were thrown in jail. The jailer locked them up in chains.

That night, Paul and Silas sat awake in

© 1995 by Phoenix Data Systems

This jail cell in Philippi is said to be where Paul and Silas once were locked in chains.

Fortune teller: Person who can tell the future by using magic

their cell. It was midnight and very dark. They were in a lot of pain. But they trusted in God. So they prayed and talked to God. Then Paul and Silas sang **hymns** of praise. The other prisoners listened to them.

This temple of Apollo was 500 years old when Paul visited Corinth. Now the ruins are over 2,500 years old!

Hymns: Songs that give honor to God

Suddenly the floor shook under Paul and Silas. The walls shook around them. An earthquake!

All the prison doors flew open. Paul's chains fell off. So did the chains on Silas and the other prisoners.

The jailer woke up. He saw the open doors. He thought all the prisoners had escaped. He felt afraid.

The Story of Paul retold, Uptton, Clive/Private Collection/© Look and Learn/The Bridgeman Art Library

God opened the doors of the jail where Paul and Silas were being kept.

He would face a terrible punishment for this. The jailer decided to kill himself with his sword.

"Don't harm yourself!" Paul called out to him. "We are all here!"[36]

The jailer was shocked. He ran into the jail and fell down at the feet of Paul and Silas. He asked them, "Sirs, what must I do to be saved?"[37]

Paul and Silas told him to believe in the Lord Jesus. So he did. Everyone in his house did too. They were baptized. "He and his whole family were filled with joy. They had become believers in God."[38]

The next day, Paul and Silas were set free from jail. They continued to travel from city to city. They encouraged the Christians. They told others about Jesus Christ. Many more people believed. But others were upset with their teachings and tried to kill them. They faced danger everywhere they went.

Finally, Paul made his way back to Jerusalem. Then he went home to Antioch. His second missionary journey had come to an end.

BIBLE HERO

Timothy—Timothy was a young man when he traveled with Paul. He was appointed as leader of the church in Ephesus. Paul wrote the letters of I Timothy and 2 Timothy to him.

EYEWITNESS ACCOUNT

Luke was an eyewitness to many things Paul did. He traveled with Paul to the city of Philippi. In Acts 16:13–14, Luke says, "On the **Sabbath** day we went outside the city gate. We walked down to the river. There we expected to find a place of prayer. We sat down and began to speak to the women who had gathered together. One of those listening was a woman named Lydia."[39]

Sabbath: In the Jewish tradition, a special day of rest from Friday sundown to Saturday sundown

BIBLE HERO

Lydia—Lydia was a businesswoman and probably very rich. She sold purple cloth. Purple was an expensive color to dye. So only the rich wore purple. Lydia became a Christian. Her house became the meeting place for the church in Philippi.

DID YOU KNOW?

Paul and Silas traveled along a very famous road called the Via Egnatia.

THE BEREANS

Paul and Silas traveled to the city of Berea. They shared the Gospel at the synagogue there. Acts 18:11–12 says, "The Bereans were very glad to receive Paul's message. They studied the Scriptures carefully every day. They wanted to see if what Paul said was true ... Many of the Jews believed. A number of important Greek women also became believers. And so did many Greek men."[40]

BIBLE HERO

Priscilla and Aquila—Priscilla and Aquila were a husband and wife team. They were tent makers, just like Paul. The local church met at their home. Paul stayed with them in Corinth for a year and a half.

Chapter 10

THE THIRD MISSIONARY JOURNEY

Once again, Paul decided to go on a trip. Once again, he wanted to return to the churches he had started. He also planned to tell even more people the news about Jesus. It would be Paul's third missionary journey.

This time Paul followed the road north. He stopped in churches along the road where he encouraged and strengthened the believers. He traveled all the way to the city of Ephesus.

Ephesus was an important city in the Roman Empire. It was the second largest city in **Asia Minor**. It was almost as big as Antioch, where Paul's home church was.

 Asia Minor: Most of the area now known as Turkey

Paul's third missionary journey was from about AD 53–57.

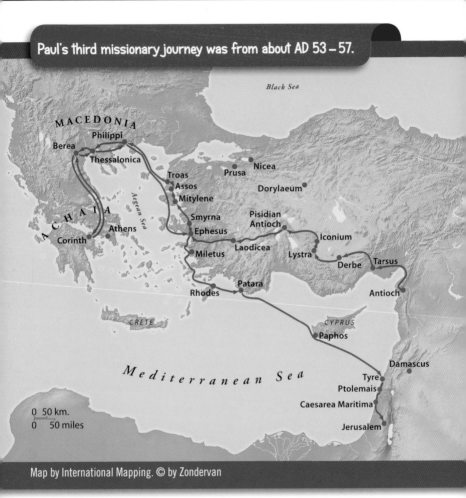

Map by International Mapping. © by Zondervan

Paul stayed in Ephesus for three years.

There didn't seem to be a church in Ephesus when Paul got there. He met twelve men who were followers of John the Baptist. Paul told them, "John baptized people, calling them to turn away from their sins. He

Visitors can see the ruins of Ephesus today.

© 2012 by Zondervan

told them to believe in the one who was coming after him. Jesus is that one."[41]

The men believed Paul's message. They were baptized in the name of Jesus. Then they received the Holy Spirit.

Paul preached boldly in Ephesus. God did many miracles through Paul while he was there. Many sick people were healed. "So all the Jews and Greeks who lived in Asia Minor heard the word of the Lord."[42]

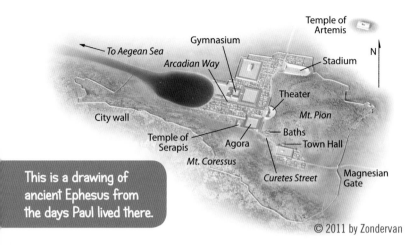

Temple of Artemis

Gymnasium

To Aegean Sea

Arcadian Way

N

Stadium

Theater

City wall

Mt. Pion

Baths

Temple of Serapis

Agora

Town Hall

Mt. Coressus

Magnesian Gate

Curetes Street

This is a drawing of ancient Ephesus from the days Paul lived there.

© 2011 by Zondervan

A large number of people in the city of Ephesus practiced magic. Their books of magic were written on scrolls. Many of these people became Christians.

One by one, they spoke up. They said how they had done evil things with their magic. But now they **repented**. They wanted to follow Jesus and do good things, not bad.

The people brought their scrolls of magic to an open area. They threw their scrolls into a large pile. "They added up the value of the scrolls. They found that it would take more than two lifetimes to earn what the scrolls were worth."[43]

Repented: Turned away from sins and turned toward God

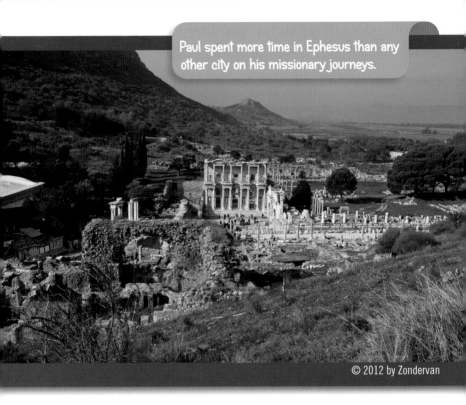

Paul spent more time in Ephesus than any other city on his missionary journeys.

Then the pile of scrolls was set on fire. The flames shot up to the sky. The heat felt intense. Many people saw the bright light of the fire.

These new believers in Ephesus stopped practicing magic. Others stopped worshiping idols all because they heard Paul's message.

Ephesus had a very famous temple in it. It was a temple for a goddess named Artemis. People came to the temple from all over the Roman Empire to worship

Artemis. This temple was one of the **Seven Wonders of the World.**

Small models were made and sold of this statue of the idol Artemis.

There was a business man in Ephesus. He made silver **models** of the temple. He sold them for a lot of money. It was a good business. But he was losing money. Not as many people were worshiping Artemis or buying silver models of the temple all because of Paul and his teachings about Jesus.

This man got very angry. He called a meeting of other businessmen. He told them how they were all losing money. Everyone got upset.

A large crowd rushed into the theater in Ephesus. They dragged two of Paul's helpers into the theater too. It was a **riot!**

It was very scary. People were angry enough to kill

© William D. Mounce

Seven Wonders of the World: The seven most amazing sites from long ago

Models: Small copies of the real thing

Riot: A large group of people start acting angry and sometimes hurt others

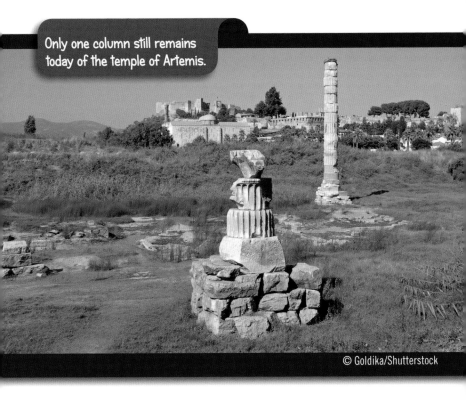

Only one column still remains today of the temple of Artemis.

© Goldika/Shutterstock

someone. Nobody knew what was going to happen. Paul wanted to speak to the crowd. But his friends told him it was safer to stay away.

Finally, a city leader spoke to the crowd. He told them to go home. They might get in trouble with the Romans. The riot came to an end. Everyone left the theater.

Finally, Paul continued on his missionary journey. On his travels, Paul wrote letters to some of the

This is the theater where the riot took place because of Paul and his teachings.

churches he couldn't visit, giving advice and teachings. Many of these letters are part of the Bible today.

Paul visited more cities and more churches. He preached everywhere he went. One time he preached all day and late into the night.

A young man sat on a window ledge to listen to

Paul. He fell asleep. Then he fell out of the window to the ground below and died.

Paul rushed down the stairs and out to the street. Paul prayed for the young man. The man came to life again. Then Paul went back to preaching. He talked the rest of the night until the sun came up.

Soon after that, Paul sailed to Jerusalem. He knew he would face danger and hardship there. Many others knew this too. Even the prophet Agabus warned Paul he would be arrested in Jerusalem.

Paul went anyway. He was willing to tell people about Jesus even if he had to suffer. His third missionary journey came to an end.

EYEWITNESS ACCOUNT

Before Paul arrived in Ephesus, there had been a different temple for Artemis. It had been destroyed by fire. Strabo wrote that a new temple had been built and "the citizens constructed one more magnificent. They collected for this purpose the **ornaments** of the women, contributions from private property, and the money arising from the sale of pillars of the former temple."[44]

Ornaments: Jewelry

BIBLE HERO

John the Baptist—John was a relative of Jesus. John called people to turn away from their sins and turn to God. He baptized them in the Jordan River. That is why he was called John the Baptist.

DID YOU KNOW?

After Paul left, the church in Ephesus grew. Young Timothy became a leader in the church of Ephesus. Paul's friends Aquila and Priscilla became part of the church in Ephesus too.

Chapter 11

APPEAL TO CAESAR

Paul was happy to be back with his friends in Jerusalem. Luke was with him again. They went to visit James and the **elders**.

Paul reported all the wonderful things God had done during his mission trips. Many people who weren't Jews had become Christians.

James and the other elders were filled with joy at this news. But they knew it was dangerous for Paul in Jerusalem. They said many people accused Paul of telling the Jews not to follow the Law of Moses. Of course this wasn't true. But that's what people thought.

Paul agreed to be careful. He agreed to go to the

Elders: Leaders of the Jews

temple and to follow certain traditions of the Jews. This would show others he lived a holy life.

Paul went to the temple with his friends. A few days later trouble started.

Some Jews were at the temple. They were visiting from Asia Minor. Paul had traveled through their cities on his missionary journeys.

This is a model of the temple in Jerusalem.

These men were upset with Paul for teaching people about Jesus. They spread lies about Paul. They stirred up the crowds. Soon there was a big riot. People came running to the temple from all over the city.

The Jewish leaders arrested Paul. The Roman soldiers marched quickly to the scene. The Roman commander took Paul away.

However, the commander allowed Paul to speak to the crowd. Paul confessed how he used to kill Christians. But then he met Jesus on the road to Damascus. He told how his life had completely changed and that he now took the Good News to people who weren't Jewish.

At these words, the crowd started shouting, "Kill him! He isn't fit to live!"[45]

The Roman commander didn't understand why the Jews were so angry with Paul. So he put Paul in prison. The next day he called together the Sanhedrin and the chief priests. He had Paul stand trial before them.

Paul knew that some members of the Sanhedrin were Pharisees. They believed in the resurrection of the dead. Paul also knew that some of them were Sadducees. They didn't believe in the resurrection of the dead.

So Paul told them that he was on trial because he believed in the resurrection of the dead.

This prompted the Pharisees and Sadducees to argue. The Pharisees thought Paul should not be punished for teaching about Jesus. The Sadducees thought he should be. They shouted and made a lot of noise. The commander thought they would kill Paul.

He ordered his soldiers to take Paul away to their fort.

That night Paul had a surprise visitor. Jesus himself appeared to Paul. Jesus said, "Be brave! You have given witness about me in Jerusalem. You must do the same in Rome."[46]

The words of Jesus encouraged Paul. Now Paul knew what God wanted him to do next. God wanted Paul to travel to Rome. There were people there who needed to hear about Jesus.

But the next day, Paul had another surprise visitor. His young nephew came to see him at the fort. He told Paul about a secret plot. Forty men had agreed to kill Paul! The plan was to hide. Then they would attack Paul on his way to see the Sanhedrin again.

Plot: Plan

Paul sent his nephew to tell this news to the Roman commander.

The commander took immediate action. He gave an order to his officers. He said, "Gather a company of 200 soldiers, 70 horsemen, and 200 men armed with spears. Get them ready to go to Caesarea at nine o'clock tonight."[47]

That night, Paul

Paul's arrest in Jerusalem

rode a horse. He was guarded by the Roman soldiers. They galloped down the road. Paul made it safely all the way to Herod's Palace in the city of Caesarea.

Providence Collection/GoodSalt

Paul was put on trial once again. He stood before the Roman governor of that area. Jewish leaders came from Jerusalem. They said things about Paul that were not true.

Nobody could make a decision about what to do with Paul. So Paul was kept in prison there for two years. Paul was able to tell the government leaders[48]

Herod's palace in Caesarea

Baker Photo Archive

about Jesus. Finally, a new governor was put in place.
Paul was brought in for a new trial.

Once again, the Jewish leaders said things about
Paul that were not true. They could not prove
anything. Then the governor asked Paul to go back to
Jerusalem. He wanted Paul to go on trial before the
Sanhedrin again.

Paul remembered that Jesus said he must go to
Rome. At that time, Rome was the most important

city in the whole world. Caesar, the ruler of the Roman Empire, was in Rome.

Paul said, "If I am guilty of anything worthy of death, I'm willing to die. But the charges brought against me by these Jews are not true. No one has

This mosaic was found on the floor of a building in Caesarea. It quotes Paul from Romans 13:3, "You don't want to be afraid of those in authority, do you? Then do what is right."

Todd Bolen/www.BiblePlaces.com

the right to hand me over to them. I make my **appeal** to Caesar!"[49]

The governor answered, "You have made an appeal to Caesar. To Caesar you will go!"[50]

Paul's next journey was about to begin. He was going to Rome.

Appeal: Ask to go to a higher court

BIBLE HERO

Paul's Nephew—Paul's nephew was young, but he was still a hero! He was the son of Paul's sister and probably lived in Jerusalem. He was very brave to talk with the commander of the Roman army and tell him about the secret plot of the Jews. He risked his own life to save the life of his uncle Paul.

EYEWITNESS ACCOUNT

The historian Josephus said Caesarea was a grand city. Josephus said Herod "set about getting a plan for a magnificent city there, and erected many **edifices** with great diligence all over it, and this of white stone. He also adorned it with most **sumptuous** palaces and large edifices for containing the people; and what was the greatest and most laborious work of all, he adorned it with a haven, that was always free from the waves of the sea."[51]

DID YOU KNOW?

Herod's Palace in Caesarea was built by Herod the Great between 25 and 13 BC. This was the same Herod who tried to kill Jesus when Jesus was born.

Edifices: Buildings
Sumptuous: Fancy

Chapter 12

FROM PAUL IN ROME

Preparations were made for Paul to sail to Rome. Before he left, however, important visitors arrived at Caesarea—King Herod and his wife.

The king and his wife went to the courtroom. All the leaders of the city were there. The governor was there too. They brought in Paul to speak to them.

Paul told them all about how Jesus had appeared to him. He explained how belief in Jesus saves people from their sins and offers hope to live a life right with God. Paul shared the Good News with the highest rulers in Israel except for Caesar himself!

After he was done, they sent Paul on a ship to Rome. He was guarded by a Roman centurion. Other

Centurion: The leader of over 100 soldiers in the Roman army

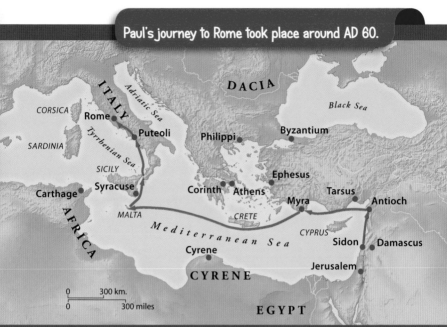

Paul's journey to Rome took place around AD 60.

prisoners were on the ship too. So were some of Paul's friends.

Winter was just starting. It was a bad time of year to sail. It was very stormy. One day the worst storm of all hit them. It was a hurricane! Everyone thought they would die at sea.

In the middle of the storm, an angel spoke to Paul. The angel said, "Do not be afraid, Paul. You must go on trial in front of Caesar. God has shown his grace by sparing the lives of all those sailing with you."[52]

Mosaic of a first-century ship.

© William D. Mounce

The ship crashed into a sandbar. It was near an island called Malta. Some people swam to shore. Others floated on boards from the broken ship. Just as the angel said, everyone was safe.

The time on Malta was important. Paul was able to tell the people on the island about Jesus. He was even bitten by a snake but didn't die. He healed many people in the name of Jesus. Everything pointed to the power of God's love.

After the winter storms were over, they sailed again toward Rome. The Christians in Rome were happy to see Paul. He was allowed to live in a house. A Roman soldier guarded him.

"For two whole years Paul stayed there in a house he rented. He welcomed all who came to see him. He preached boldly about God's kingdom. No one could keep him from teaching people about the Lord Jesus Christ."[53]

Luke did not write about what happened next to Paul. The book of Acts ends with Paul in Rome.

Was Paul set free? Did he travel to Spain and share the Gospel there? Did he stay in Rome under Roman guard?

Wikimedia Commons

Nero condemned both Paul and Peter to death.

Nobody knows for sure. It was during these years, however, that Paul continued to write letters with messages about Jesus. He wrote letters to young pastors Timothy and Titus. He told them to follow the teachings of Jesus. He told them not to listen to false teachings.

A new emperor came to power in Rome during Paul's life. Nero became Caesar. Nero made it against the law to be a Christian.

Tradition says that Paul was killed by Nero around 67 AD. This happened because Paul was a Christian. He became a martyr just like Stephen so many years earlier.

Paul taught that when a Christian died, he went to live in heaven with Jesus. Paul's life had come to an end on earth. But now he lived in heaven forever.

Paul spent his last days in this dungeon in Rome.

Baker Photo Archive

Paul's voice could no longer be heard preaching in the synagogues or teaching the Gentiles about Jesus. But Paul was not silent. People read his letters aloud in church meetings.

People can still read Paul's words today. His letters are part of the Bible's New Testament. People still learn from Paul the truth about Jesus and his teachings.

Paul gave his life to tell others about Jesus. He shared the good news about Jesus with people of his generation. In the years after that, new generations of people read Paul's testimony and became Christians. Paul's words are still changing the world today.

DID YOU KNOW?

Paul told the Gospel to King Herod Agrippa II. He was the great-grandson of King Herod the Great.

EYEWITNESS ACCOUNT

Luke sailed with Paul on his trip to Rome. He was an eyewitness to all that happened on the trip. In Acts 27:14–15, he tells about the hurricane. Luke says, "The sun and stars didn't appear for many days. The storm was terrible. So we gave up all hope of being saved."[54]

PAUL'S FINAL WORDS

Some of Paul's last words were written in a letter to Timothy. In 2 Timothy 4:7, Paul says, "I have fought the good fight. I have finished the race. I have kept the faith."[55]

EYEWITNESS ACCOUNT

Christians like Paul were put on trial in the Roman Court. Pliny the Younger was a Roman ruler living about 50 years after Paul. He wrote to the emperor for instructions on what to do with Christians. In his letter he wrote, "I now handle it this way with those who are turned over to me as Christians. I ask them directly, in person, if they are Christian. I ask a second and third time to be sure, and indicate to them the danger of their situation."[56] If they still said they are Christian, Pliny ordered them taken away to be killed.

TIMELINE OF PAUL
(some dates are approximate)

© Wikimedia Commons

© Standard Publishing/GoodSalt

35 AD
Paul becomes a Christian

50 AD
Paul speaks at Jerusalem Council

© Wikimedia Commons

Wikimedia Commons

46–48 AD
Paul's first missionary
journey

50–52 AD
Paul's second missionary
journey

WORLD HISTORY

32 AD
Church at Rome started

30 AD
Death and resurrection of Jesus

© Wikimedia Commons

53–57 AD
Paul's third
missionary journey

© ruskpp/Shutterstock

59 AD
Paul's journey to Rome

© Wikimedia Commons

57 AD
Paul arrested
in Jerusalem

© Wikimedia Commons

67 AD
Paul killed by Nero

54 AD– 68 AD
Nero is emperor of
Roman Empire

58 AD– 76 AD
Ming-Ti is
emperor of China

70 AD
Temple in Jerusalem
destroyed by Rome

GLOSSARY

Christ: The Greek word for Messiah

Christians: People who believe in Jesus Christ and his teachings

Conversion: The experience when someone decides to believe that Jesus is God

Cross: Two pieces of wood put together in the shape of a T that Romans used to kill people by hanging them on it

Devil: Satan, the enemy of God and the spirit of evil

Essenes: Jewish group who wrote the Dead Sea Scrolls

Eyewitness: Person who actually saw something happen

False teachers: People who taught things the Bible did not teach

Feasts: Important holidays celebrated by the Jews

Gentiles: People who aren't Jews

God's grace: Giving the free gift of salvation without following rules to earn it

Good News: The news that Jesus is the Messiah, the Christ

Gospel: Word meaning "good news," each of the first four books of the New Testament

Greek: The language the New Testament was written in

Hebrew: The language of the Jews, another name for a Jew

High priest: The leader of all the priests

Holy Spirit: The Spirit of God

Hymns: Songs that give honor to God

Idols: Statues that people worship

Jerusalem Council: A special meeting of the early church that decided salvation was a free gift from God to those who believe in Jesus

Law of Moses: The first five books in the Bible that have the Ten Commandments

Martyr: Person who is killed for his faith

Messiah: The promised deliverer of the Jews

Miracles: Amazing events that only God could have done

Missionaries: People who take a message of faith to others

Persecution: Hurting or killing people because of their beliefs

Pharisee: Jewish group who followed traditions they made up

Prophets: People who tell God's words to others

Psalms: Poems and songs in the Bible written mostly by King David

Rabbi: A teacher

Repented: Turned away from sins and turned toward God

Resurrection: When Jesus rose from the dead and came alive again

Sabbath: A special day of rest from Friday sundown to Saturday sundown

Sacrifices: Special gifts to God such as an animal or grain

Sadducees: Jewish group who was strict about following God's Law, but did not follow the traditions of the Pharisees

Salvation: Saving from punishment for sins

Sanhedrin: The highest group of Jewish leaders who met in Jerusalem and made important decisions

Savior: The One who saves people from getting punished for their sins

Sins: Bad things people think, say, or do

Son of God: A title for Jesus meaning he is the Messiah

Son of Man: A title Jesus used to show that even though he was God, he had come to earth as a man

Synagogue: Building where Jews meet for worship

Ten Commandments: Ten holy laws given by God to the Jews

SELECTED BIBLIOGRAPHY

Alexander, David and Pat. *Zondervan Handbook to the Bible*. Grand Rapids, Michigan: Zondervan, 2002.

"Antiquities of the Jews," *The Works of Flavius Josephus*, December 21, 2013, http://www.sacred-texts.com/jud/josephus/index.htm.

Campbell, Charlie H. Archaeological Evidence for the Bible: Exciting Discoveries Verifying Persons, Places and Events in the Bible. Carlsbad, California: The Always Be Ready Apologetics Ministry, 2012.

Campbell, Charlie H. *One Minute Answers to Skeptics' Top Forty Questions*. United States: Aquintas Publishing, 2005.

Connelly, Douglas. Amazing Discoveries that Unlock the Bible: A Visual Experience. Grand Rapids, Michigan: Zondervan, 2008.

Free, Joseph P. and Howard F. Vos. *Archaeology and Bible History*. Grand Rapids, Michigan: Zondervan, 1992.

Gardner, Paul D. *New International Encyclopedia of Bible Characters*. Grand Rapids, Michigan: Zondervan, 1995.

Gower, Ralph. The New Manners and Customs of Bible Times. Chicago: Moody Press, 1987.

House, H. Wayne. Zondervan Charts: Chronological and Background Charts of the New Testament. Grand Rapids: Michigan, 2009.

Matthews, Victor H. *Manners and Customs in the Bible*. Peabody, Massachusetts: Hendrickson Publishers, 1991.

Missler, Chuck. *Learn the Bible in 24 Hours*. Nashville: Thomas Nelson Publishers, 2002.

"Pliny and the Christians, Translated by William Harris,{dec63} Prof. Em. Middlebury College,{dec63}www.middlebury.edu/~harris," May 24, 2013, http://community.middlebury.edu/~harris/Classics/plinytrajan.html.

Rasmussen, Carl G. *Zondervan Atlas of the Bible*. Grand Rapids: Zondervan, 2010.

Silva, Moisé and J.D. Douglas and Merrill C. Tenney. *Zondervan Illustrated Bible Dictionary*. Grand Rapids, Michigan: Zondervan, 2011.

"Strabo's Geography, Books XI through XVII, Translated from Greek by W. Falconer," May 22, 2013, http://rbedrosian.com/Classic/strabo.html.

Strobel, Lee. *The Case for the Resurrection*. Grand Rapids, Michigan: Zondervan, 2009.

Tenney, Merrill C., General Editor. *The Zondervan Encyclopedia of the Bible, Volumes 1 – 5*. Grand Rapids, Michigan: Zondervan, 2009.

"The Life of Flavius Josephus, 2," *The Works of Flavius Josephus*, May 26, 2013, http://www.sacred-texts.com/jud/josephus/autobiog.htm.

"The Wars of the Jews," *The Works of Flavius Josephus*, April 6, 2013, http://www.sacred-texts.com/jud/josephus/index.htm.

Vos, Howard F. *Nelson's New Illustrated Bible Manners & Customs*. Nashville: Thomas Nelson, 1999.

Walker, Peter. *In the Steps of Paul*. Grand Rapids, Michigan: Zondervan, 2008.

Walton, John H., Mark L. Strauss, and Ted Cooper Jr. *The Essential Bible Companion*. Grand Rapids, Michigan: Zondervan, 2006.

SOURCE NOTES

1. "Strabo's Geography, Books XI through XVII, Chapter 5.13, Translated from Greek by W. Falconer," May 21, 2013, http://rbedrosian.com/Classic/strabo14e.htm.

2. Campbell, Charlie H. *Archaeological Evidence for the Bible: Exciting Discoveries Verifying Persons, Places and Events in the Bible.* Carlsbad, California: The Always Be Ready Apologetics Ministry, 2012, page 130.

3. Exodus 20, NIrV

4. Acts 22:3, NIrV

5. Acts 9:2, NIrV

6. Acts 6:14, NIrV

7. Acts 7:52, NIrV

8. "The Life of Flavius Josephus, 2," *The Works of Flavius Josephus*, May 26, 2013, http://www.sacred-texts.com/jud/josephus/autobiog.htm.

9. Luke 24:18, NIrV

10. Acts 22:7, NIrV

11. Acts 9:5, NIrV

12. Acts 9:6, NIrV

13. Galatians 1:13, NIrV

14. Acts 9:15, NIrV

15. 1 Corinthians 15:3–8, NIrV

16. John 20:29, NIrV

17. Acts 9:21, NIrV

18. "Strabo's Geography, Books XVI, Chapter 2.20, Translated from Greek by W. Falconer," May 27, 2013, http://rbedrosian. com/Classic/strabo16c.htm.

19. Isaiah 53:4–5, NIrV

20. Acts 9:15, NIrV

21. Acts 13:2, NIrV

22. "Strabo's Geography, Books XVI, Chapter 2.5, Translated from Greek by W. Falconer," May 27, 2013, http://rbedrosian. com/Classic/strabo16b.htm.

23. Acts 13:10, NIrV

24. Acts 13:11, NIrV

25. Acts 14:15, NIrV

26. Acts 13:38–39, NIrV

27. Acts 1:8, NIrV

28. Acts 15:1, NIrV

29. Acts 15:5, NIrV

30. Acts 15:10–11, NIrV

31. Acts 15:19, NIrV

32. Acts 15:36, NIrV

33. Romans 3:22–24, NIrV

34. Acts 16:20, NIrV

35. Acts 16:20, NIrV

36. Acts 16:28, NIrV

37. Acts 16:30, NIrV

38. Acts 16:34, NIrV

39. Acts 16:13–14, NIrV

40. Acts 18:11–12, NIrV

41. Acts 19:4, NIrV

42. Acts 19:10, NIrV

43. Acts 19:19, NIrV

44. "Strabo's Geography, Books XIV, Chapter 1.22, Translated from Greek by W. Falconer," May 22, 2013, http://rbedrosian.com/Classic/strabo14.htm.

45. Acts 22:22, NIrV

46. Acts 23:11, NIrV

47. Acts 23:23, NIrV

48. Romans 13:3, NIrV

49. Acts 25:11, NIrV

50. Acts 25:12, NIrV

51. "Antiquities of the Jews," *The Works of Flavius Josephus*, 15.9.6 May 23, 2013, http://www.sacred-texts.com/jud/josephus/ant – 15.htm

52. Acts 27:24, NIrV

53. Acts 28:30–31, NIrV

54. Acts 27:20, NIrV

55. 2 Timothy 4:7, NIrV

56. "Pliny and the Christians, Translated by William Harris,–Prof. Em. Middlebury College,–www.middlebury.edu/~harris," May 24, 2013, http://community.middlebury.edu/~harris/Classics/plinytrajan.html.

STUDENT RESOURCES

Blankenbaker, Frances. *What the Bible Is All About for Young Explorers*. Ventura, California: Regal Books, 1986.

Dowley, Tim. *The Student Bible Atlas*. Minneapolis: Augsburg, 1996.

Ham, Ken with Cindy Malott, *The Answers Book for Kids, Volume 1: 22 Questions from Kids on Creation and the Fall*. Green Forest, Arizona: Master Books, 2008.

Ham, Ken with Cindy Malott, *The Answers Book for Kids, Volume 3: 22 Questions from Kids on God and the Bible*. Green Forest, Arizona: Master Books, 2009.

Ham, Ken with Cindy Malott, *The Answers Book for Kids, Volume 4: 22 Questions from Kids on Sin, Salvation, and the Christian Life*. Green Forest, Arizona: Master Books, 2009.

McDowell, Josh and Sean McDowell. *Jesus is Alive! Evidence for the Resurrection for Kids*. Ventura, California: Regal, 2009.

Osborne, Rick and K. Christie Bowler. *I Want to Know About God, Jesus, the Bible, and Prayer*. Grand Rapids, Michigan: Zonderkidz, 2000.

Strobel, Lee with Rob Suggs and Robert Elmer. *Case for Christ for Kids*. Grand Rapids, Michigan: Zonderkidz, 2010.

Van der Maas, Ruth, Marnie Wooding, and Rick Osborne. *Kid Atlas: Important Places in the Bible and Where to Find Them*. Grand Rapids, Michigan: Zonderkidz, 2002.

Water, Mark. *The Big Book About Jesus.* Nashville: Thomas Nelson Publishers, 1995.

Water, Mark. *The Big Book of Bible People.* Nashville: Thomas Nelson Publishers, 1996.

Water, Mark. *The Children's Bible Encyclopedia.* Owing Mills, Maryland: Baker, 1998.

Water, Mark. *The Children's Encyclopedia of Bible Times.* Grand Rapids, Michigan: ZondervanPublishingHouse, 1995.

ABOUT
THE AUTHOR

Nancy I. Sanders is the bestselling children's author of over 80 books including *Old Testament Days: An Activity Guide* with over 80 hands-on projects. Her award-winning nonfiction children's books include *D is for Drinking Gourd: An African American Alphabet*, *America's Black Founders*, and *Frederick Douglass for Kids*. Nancy delights in making history come alive to young readers. She lives with her husband, Jeff, and their two cats in sunny southern California. Nancy and Jeff have two grown sons, Dan and Ben (with his lovely wife Christina). Visit Nancy's website at www.nancyisanders.com.

Jesus

Get to Know Series

Nancy I. Sanders

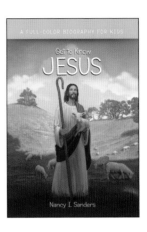

Jesus—part of the Get to Know series—is a unique biography about Jesus, the son of God. Focusing on the life and character of this biblical hero, using color photographs, maps, and other visual resources to tell the whole story, young biography fans will come to learn more about this man of God and the role he plays in history.

Featuring a bibliography and scriptural references throughout, this is sure to become a favorite for young readers and for first book reports.

Available in stores and online!

Mary
Get to Know Series

Nancy I. Sanders

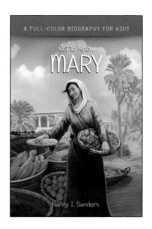

Mary—part of the Get to Know series—will teach you everything you need to know about this young woman whom God used to do great things! Mary was more than the mother of Jesus. She was a hero of the Bible. She said "Yes!" to God. Learn about Mary and her exciting place in history. Discover what it was like to grow up in Israel and be a part of Jesus' life on earth.

Featuring a bibliography and scriptural references throughout, this is sure to become a favorite for young readers and for first book reports.

King David

Get to Know Series

Nancy I. Sanders

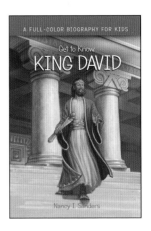

King David—part of the Get to Know series—will teach you everything you need to know about an imperfect young man whom God used to do great things! David lived an adventurous life. He protected his family's sheep from lions and bears. He fought a giant with just a sling and stone. He even spent years hiding from men who were trying to kill him. And eventually, David became a great king. But David was also a man of God. Learn more about this hero from the Bible and his exciting place in history. Discover what it was like to grow up in ancient Israel and then be a king of God's people.

Featuring a bibliography and scriptural references throughout, this is sure to become a favorite for young readers and for first book reports.

Available in stores and online!

Apostle Paul

Get to Know Series

Nancy I. Sanders

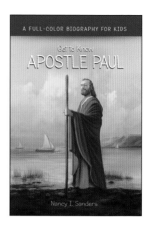

Apostle Paul—part of the Get to Know series—is a unique biography about Paul. Focusing on the life and character of this Biblical hero, using color photographs, maps, and other visual resources to tell the whole story, young biography fans will come to learn more about this man of the God, his writings, his impact on the early church, and the role he plays in history.

Featuring a bibliography and scriptural references throughout, this is sure to become a favorite for young readers and for first book reports.

Available in stores and online!